MACHINE STITCHES

MACHINE STITCHES

ANNE BUTLER
Photographs by
TERRY WADDINGTON

B T BATSFORD LTD London

First published 1976
ISBN 0 7136 3150 4

Printed in Great Britain by
The Anchor Press, Tiptree, Essex
for the publishers
B T Batsford Limited
4 Fitzhardinge Street
London W1H 0AH

CONTENTS

ACKNOWLEDGEMENT

We would like to thank all those who so readily gave us permission to use their work in this book; also the following: Mr Ralph Downing, Head of the Department of Textiles/Fashion, Manchester Polytechnic; students of the Embroidery School, Manchester Polytechnic; Mr Clarke, Bernina agent in Stockport; and the Bernina Sewing Machine Company.

AB and TW

INTRODUCTION

The purpose of this book is to show the basic effects which can be achieved using a modern domestic sewing machine.

All the examples shown in this book can be worked on a zigzag/straight stitch domestic machine. I would stress that these examples are only starting points. There are obviously many more effects which can be produced. It is the manipulation of the machine tension or speed, the use of a variety of fabrics as they differ, and attachments which allow for such a variety to be achieved.

Once the stitches are mastered they can be used either on their own or linked with hand embroidery.

Technical details

Speed Most new sewing machines have a maximum and a minimum speed switch. It is most important to learn to control the full range of speed, from no movement to very fast, by the pressure of the foot on the foot control.

Movement of the fabric In free machining, when perhaps producing circular and linear movements, the appearance of the machine stitch will be affected. The speed of moving the hands and the speed of the sewing machine also have an effect on the stitch produced as the stitch length is made by this movement.

Tension (top and bottom) For ordinary use the top and bottom tensions are matched equally, alterations being made according to the thickness of the fabric, etc. To produce a whip stitch, however, tighten the top tension and loosen (or leave as normal) the bottom tension; the bottom thread will come up and the top thread will be very taut, thus forming the whip stitch.

Needles and spool cases The size of needle, etc, will depend on the type of technique and fabric(s) that are used; as for spool cases, it is my advice to keep two, so that one can be left with the tension on it always the same, and the other can be altered when necessary. The bottom tension can be loosened and tightened to affect the stitch being made.

The stitch length and width There is a knob on the machine to set the stitch length, and a dial which can graduate the width of the stitch from straight stitch to zigzag. Obviously, by adjusting the length and width of the stitch different effects can be achieved. (Illustration 29).

Foot lever and teeth The foot lever must be lowered whether the foot is on or not; the teeth must usually be up when the foot is on and lowered when the foot is off. Throughout the book the directive 'teeth lowered' is stated when they are to be lowered, otherwise it is assumed that the teeth are up as for normal sewing.

Attachments There are many extra needles, feet, and equipment such as a rug fork, which can be bought to extend the effects which the machine can produce. The needles can be single, twin or tripple, and have different sizes and shapes to correspond with the fabric being used, the thickness of the work, and the special effect to be achieved.

Free machining This is a term used often in the book to indicate that the foot must not be used, the teeth must be dropped, and the foot lever lowered. Also, the fabric is most often in a machine-embroidery frame, especially when one is starting to master this method. There are however fabrics like vanishing muslin and iron-on *vilene* which, when put behind the fabric to be worked, make the surface taut enough to be machined without a frame. Eventually the fabric can be held taut with the fingers, but for beginners it is better to use a frame to move the fabric. To start with use the correct, equal tension, and then alter the tension (Illustration 2);

move the frame around, trying all possible movements and directions; also draw in some movements, with pencil, to see the amount of control one has and can achieve. There are many points which can go wrong: for example, if the fabric is moved too quickly the needle will bend and break on the plate; if the fabric is not moved quickly enough the thread will build up in one place and so break the needle. Generally it is good to use a medium speed, and relax!

Lines, areas, pattern and texture—these are words to keep in mind and aims to achieve by the machine, so that its potential is fully explored and it is not just used to draw with, in imitation and quickening of hand-embroidery techniques.

Equipment and materials Circular and oval frames of different diameters are made in metal and wood, and it is important to choose the appropriate size for the work in hand. It is best to bind the frame with a strip of fabric (like a 25 mm (1 in.) bandage), so that the frame does not leave circular or oval marks on the fabric. (Illustration 74).

Scissors It is advisable to keep a different pair of scissors for fabric and paper, and to have a large and small pair for cutting and fine cutting respectively. A pair of pinking scissors can be useful in order to make a different edge of the fabric.

Most machines have an unpicker supplied with them, which, as the name suggests, can be used for unpicking stitches.

Fabrics such as iron-on *vilene*, vanishing muslin, quilting fabrics, loose hessian, canvas, net, organdie— and threads such as various types of cottons, shaded cottons, metallic threads, elastic and piping cord—are used often, and are easily obtained.

Unlikely materials have also been used, such as wire, paper, and polythene. There are also fabrics which can be dissolved by an acetate; thus some of the machine effects in this book can be worked and the fabric then dissolved away, leaving the machine work to be applied to or suspended in another fabric.

Techniques It is very interesting to observe how many of the machine techniques are similar to hand techniques, often being simply a quicker way of producing

right Stretching fabric on a board

the latter. Such techniques covered in this book are—edges, seams, patchwork, gold work, inlay, three types of quilting, piping, appliqué, holding down threads (couching, etc), pulled work (machining on loose hessian), rugging, darning, whipping threads, shadow work, net darning, smocking (gathers), canvas work. Combined with hand embroidery, these machine methods can become richer and stronger; the reverse also applies.

Stretching If, when the machining is finished, the work is gathered where it should be flat, then the fabric will have to be stretched. In order to do this cover a board with cork. Soak in water a piece of soft absorbent fabric, remove the excess water in a spin dryer, and stretch the cloth on the board surface. Then lay the machined fabric face up on the cloth and stretch it flat, holding it with drawing pins. When it is dry, the drawing pins can be removed and the work is ready to be mounted.

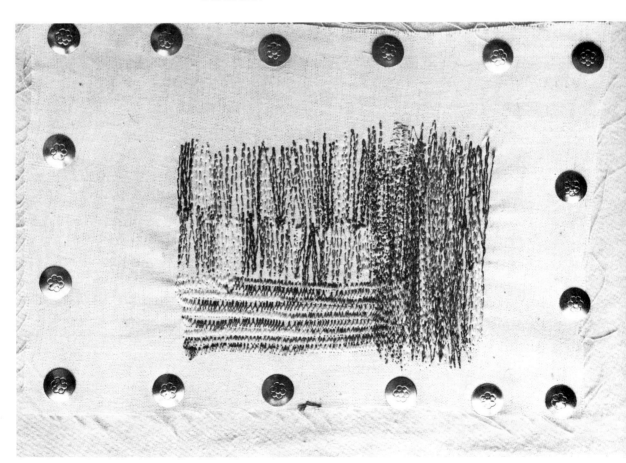

STRAIGHT STITCH

Please note that where there is no mention with the
captions that the work is free machining (no foot) and a
foot has been used, it will be an embroidery foot (or a
zigzag foot will perhaps at times be more suitable).

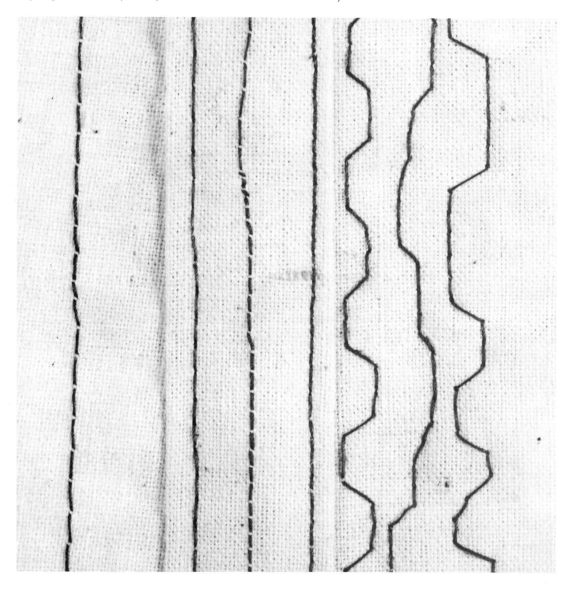

1 *left* Straight stitch: variations with the stitch length and moving the needle from side to side

2 Straight stitch: variations with the top tension too tight and the bottom tension too loose. Free machining worked in a frame. In this example different movements have been made which affect the appearance of the uneven tension. If the bottom tension needs to be even looser the tension spring on the spool case can be altered

3 Straight stitch: top tension too tight and the bottom too loose. Free machining in a frame. Movements in the machined area shown when the bottom thread has pulled up further than usual when a change of direction has been made   Irene Bobkiewicz

4 Straight stitch: top tension too tight and the bottom too loose. Free machining in a frame. A whole area made with a simple rhythmic movement of the fabric being machined   Irene Bobkiewicz

5 Straight stitch: top
tension too tight and the
bottom too loose. The top
and bottom threads are
different colours, so the
stitch looks whipped. Free
machining in a frame
Maria Theresa Fernandes

6 Straight stitch: top
tension too tight and the
bottom too loose. The
diamond shape is worked in
the opposite direction. Free
machining in a frame
Janis Riley

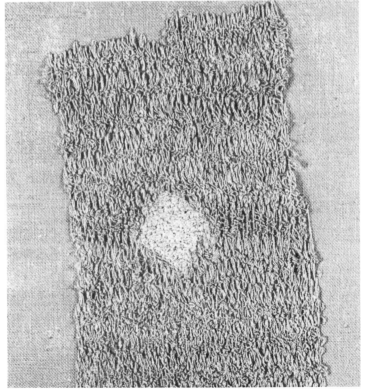

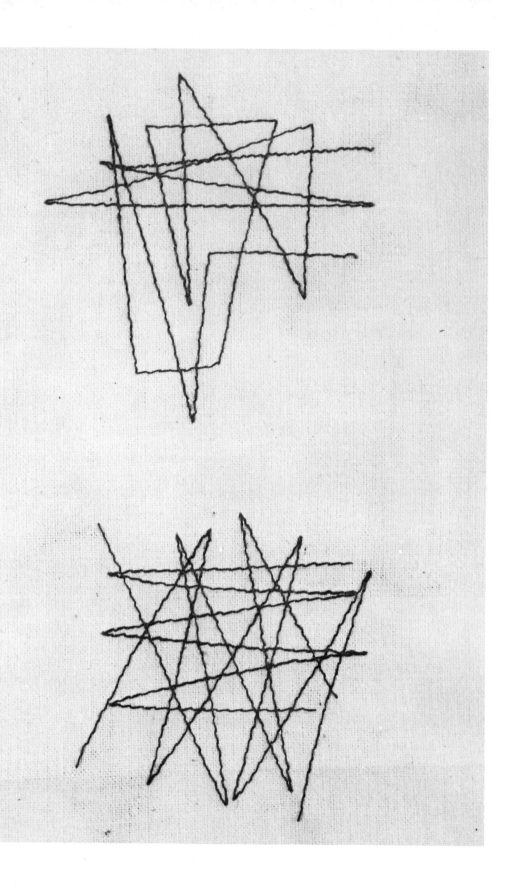

7 *left* Straight stitch. The change in the direction of stitches has been made by leaving the needle in the fabric, lifting the foot and turning the fabric, (the reverse could also be used). The tension must be correct or the work will pucker

8 *right* Straight stitch lines holding together rows of ribbons, braids and bias binding; note the machine lines continue into the gaps between the fabrics
Beverly Whitehead

9 Irregular thick threads held down with a straight stitch down the centre

10 Straight stitch: a diagonal movement making the filling of the square. Correct tension, and free machining in a frame   Irene Bobkiewicz

11 *left* Straight stitch on a cord fabric with correct tension. The vertical movement blocks worked first, diagonal movement on top next   Irene Bobkiewicz

12 *right* Straight stitch: machine cotton on top and different threads (too thick to go through the eye of the needle), have been wound by hand on to the bottom spool. The work is machined upside down so the spool threads will be on top. Machining in a frame. Tensions have been varied as well as types of thread and speed of machining

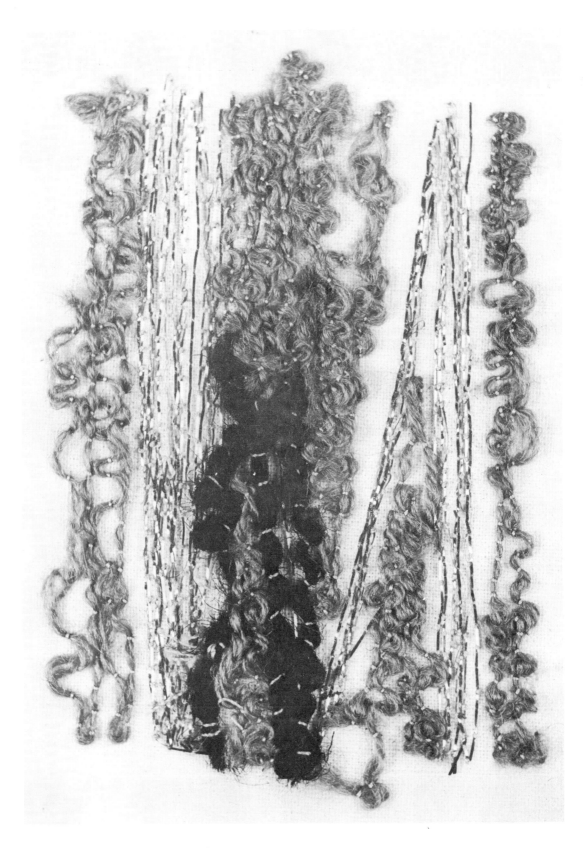

13 Three stages to produce the small piece which could be applied flower centres — other shapes can be made using this method.
1 Machine three times around making a circle
2 Cut a circle out larger than the machined one
3 Cut the outside shape, and have a centre in another fabric.
Wool darning foot and straight stitch

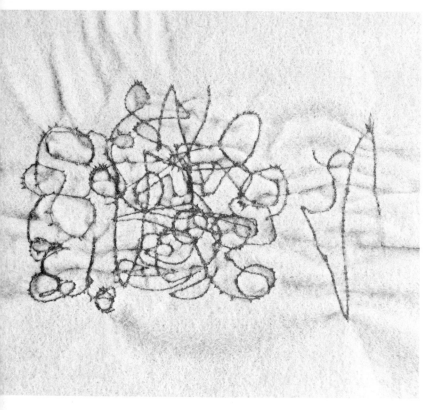

14 *left* A soft fabric with a straight stitch and very tight top tension. Free machining

15 *right* Free machining in a frame: the machine work making the negative area rather than the positive

16 *left* Dyes and felt tip pens have been used to pattern flower shapes on a large piece of fabric, straight stitch machining has then been added, free machining in a frame. The shapes have been cut out, the edges turned under and glued, and assembled to make a repeat pattern   Philippa Bergson

17 *below* Calico fabric has been ironed onto a piece of *vilene*, the strips measured onto the back and cut out with a knife. The strips have been turned over at the edges and machined with a straight stitch. The background calico has been ironed onto a piece of *vilene*, measured, and the cuts made with a knife. The strips have been woven through the background fabric   Margaret Murray

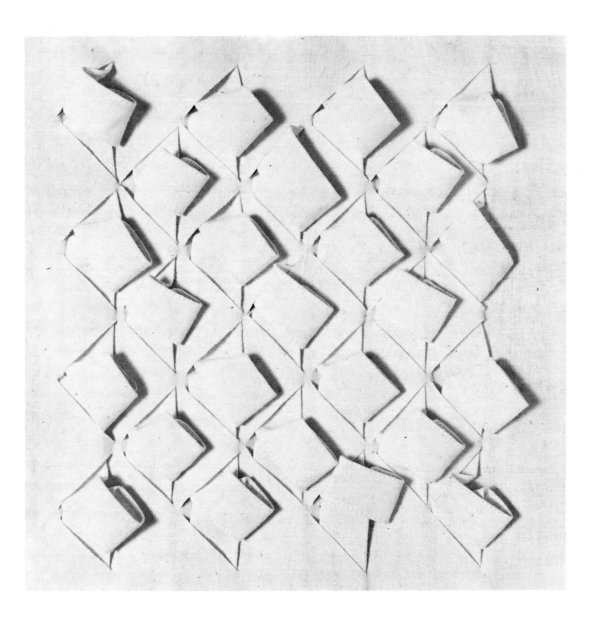

18 Straight stitch can obviously be used to link fabrics together, here an ordinary seam links strips of fabric together

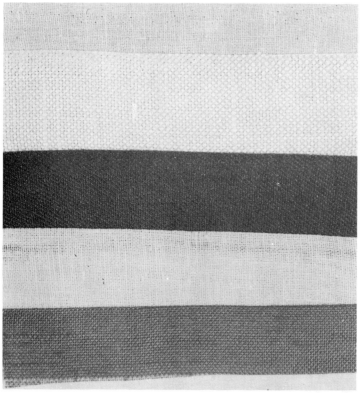

19 The seam made in 18 is opened out and pressed

20, 21 and 22 Here the
fabric produced in 18 and
19 is used as a background
fabric for small samples
Helyn Kenyon

23 A fabric made as in 18
and 19 is cut into strips to
make a fabric, 24

24 The strips made in 23
are reassembled to form a
patchwork fabric

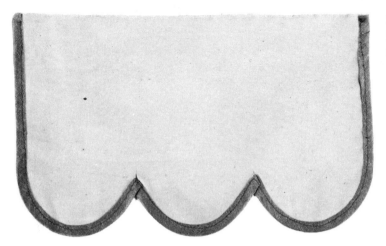

25 Two fabric shapes have been cut identically, and edged with a bias binding Beverly Whitehead

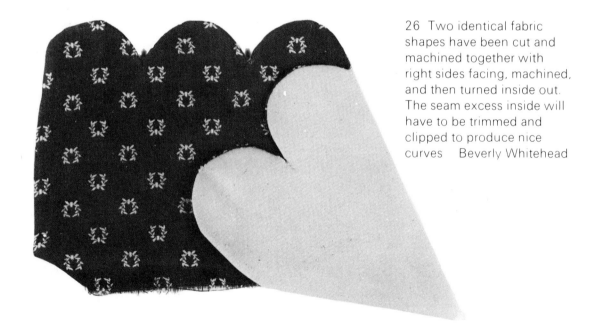

26 Two identical fabric shapes have been cut and machined together with right sides facing, machined, and then turned inside out. The seam excess inside will have to be trimmed and clipped to produce nice curves   Beverly Whitehead

27 False seams have been made by machining a whole piece of fabric. On the right side the effect is like a seam

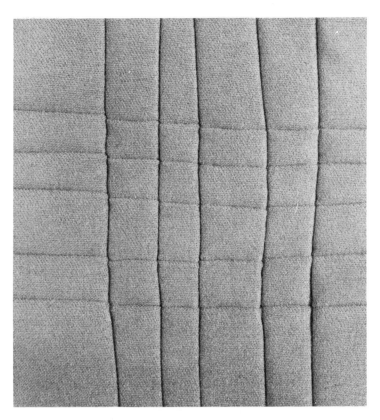

28 This is the reverse side of 27, and the ridged effect can be used as well as the right side

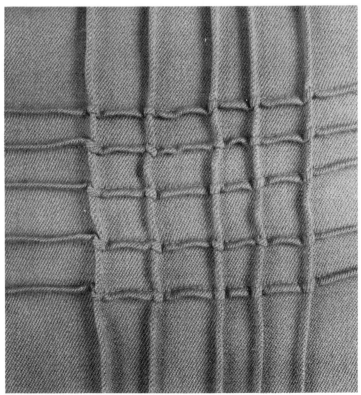

ZIGZAG STITCH

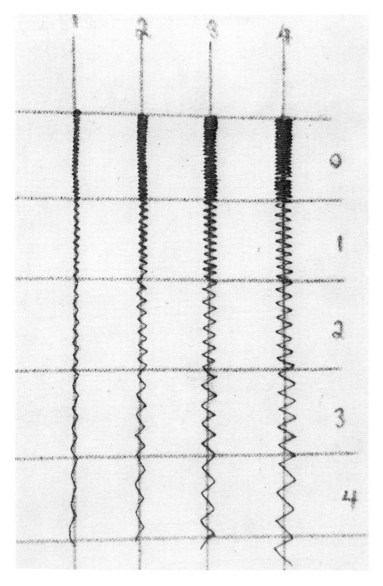

29 The top numbers indicate the width of the stitch from 1 to 4, and the numbers on the right hand side the length of the stitch from 0 to 4. The full range of the zigzag stitch. The knob has been turned while the machine is working

30 *opposite page* These examples show the free use of the width of the zigzag stitch (29), quickly moving the lever from 1 to 4 and back again to make these shapes   Audrey Wynne

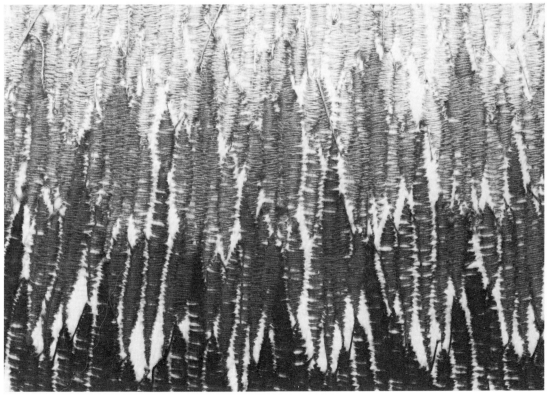

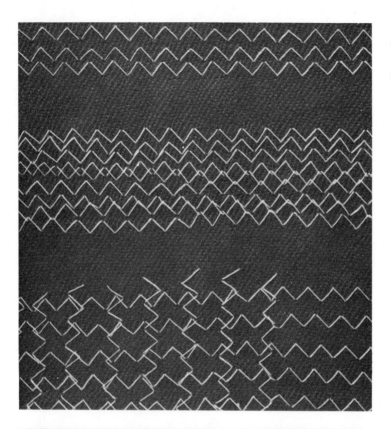

31 This sample shows the simple rhythms and patterns which can be made with a zigzag stitch—of course many more are possible

32 Same stitch as in 31 but here the lines go back and across each other

33 The top area is worked with an ordinary foot, etc, and the bottom free machining with a frame. They both are made using two different coloured cotton threads through a single needle

34 Darning foot in a frame. The colour of the thread corresponds to the word, eg 'RED' is in a red thread Beverly Whitehead

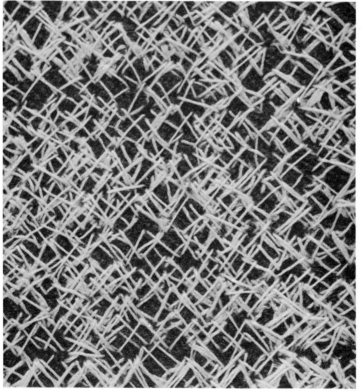

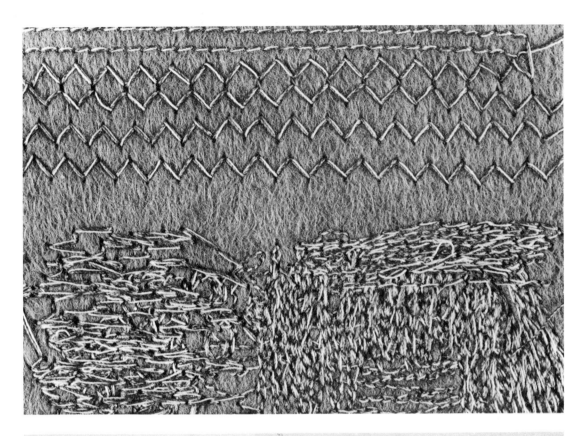

35 Zigzag stitch, free machining in a frame, no foot. The machine is allowed to make a clump and then moved on to make the next one. In this sample some clumps have been cut with an unpicker to make a fluffy surface

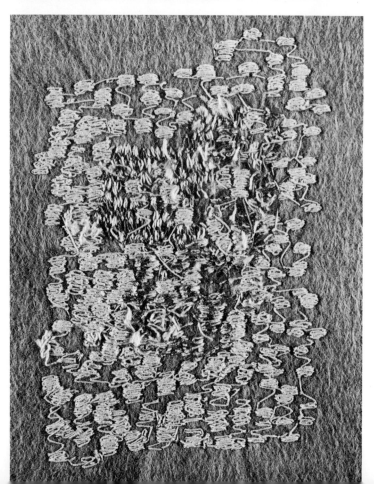

36 The back of 35 shows how quite often the back of a machine work is as interesting as the front

37 *right* Zigzag stitch, free machining in a frame. A clump made with the zigzag and then the machine stitching point moved quite a distance so that there is a long line of thread between clumps, (release thread carefully so as not to bend the needle). Tensions can be altered and the scale of the clump changed

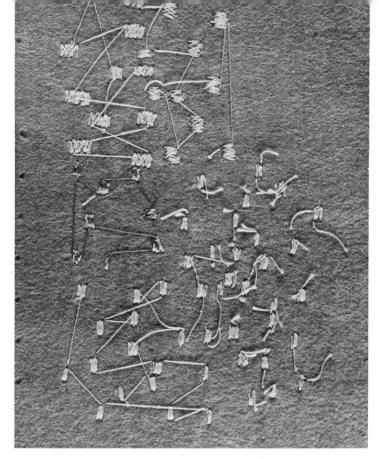

38 *below* Blocks of close zigzag stitch in various colours are used here to hold down patterned cotton squares   Philippa Bergson

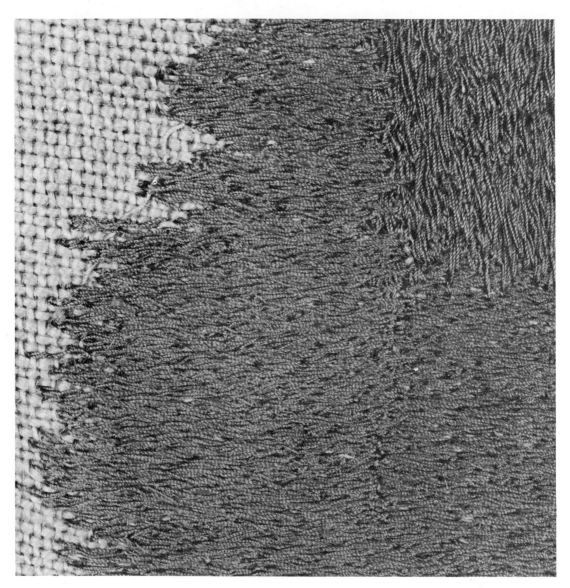

39 A No. 4 zigzag stitch
setting, free machining, in a
frame. The fabric has been
pulled in the direction of the
stitches and this movement
is possible to do with a
vertical or horizontal
movement of the fabric
being machined Maria
Theresa Fernandes

40 Free machining, in a
frame, a small zigzag stitch.
Zigzag lines using shaded
cotton thread

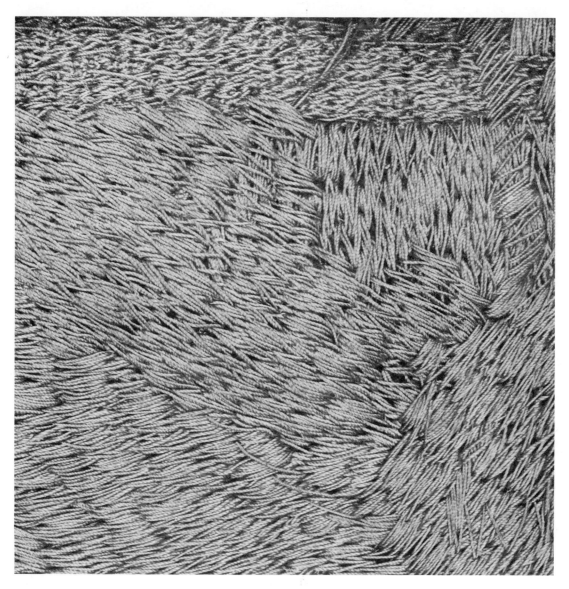

41 Free machining, in a
frame, a large zigzag stitch
Maria Theresa Fernandes

42 Close rows of zigzag,
made with a frequent change
in the colour of cotton being
used   Beryl Patten

43 The back of 42

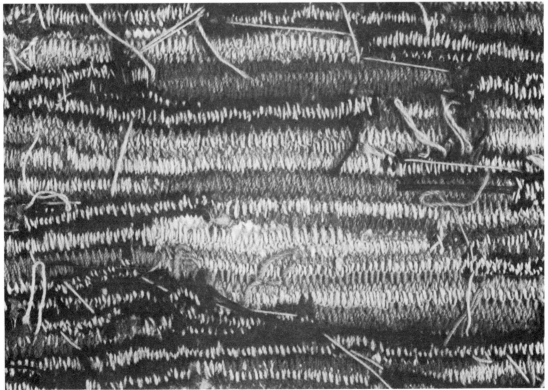

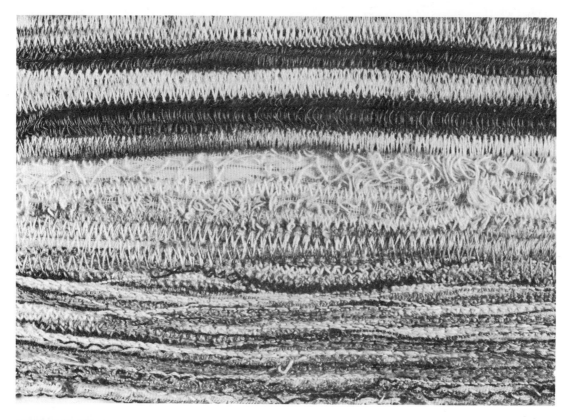

44 *above* Various widths
of zigzag stitch have been
worked in separate rows and
on top of each other
Beryl Patten

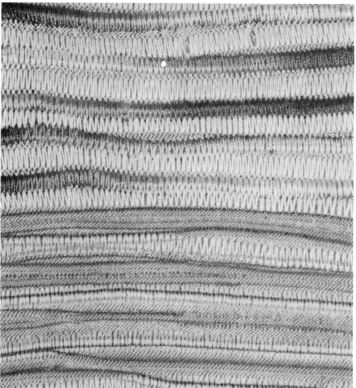

45 *left* Rows of zigzag
stitch made using a shaded
cotton thread   Beryl Patten

46 *right* Zigzag stitch, the rows have been worked one way and then the other way, on a velvet fabric. Irene Hobson

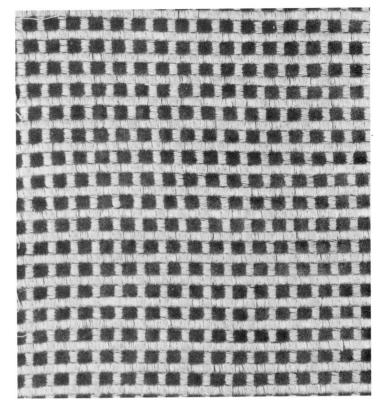

47 *below* This example is made by first making a fabric as in 63. This has then been cut either side of the zigzag stitch lines and woven to form another effect entirely Irene Hobson

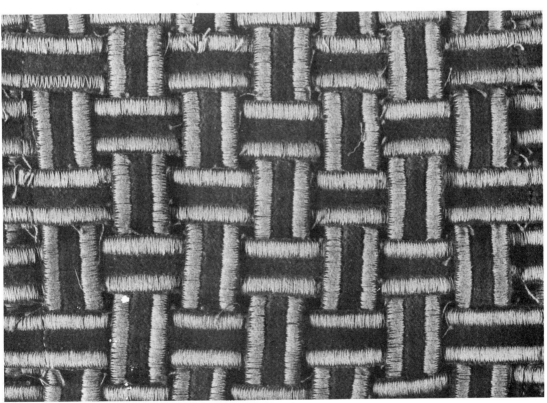

48 Zigzag stitch lines on a
suede fabric making an all
over pattern   Helen Lord

49 Zigzag stitch lines used
to appliqué zigzag gingham
fabric lines

ZIGZAG STITCH AND STRAIGHT STITCH

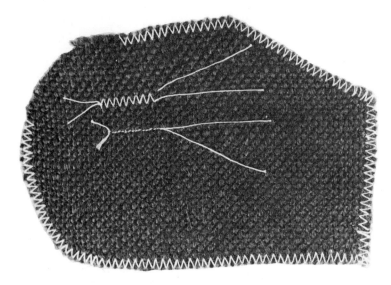

50 This example shows how to hold down a piece of appliqué with a zigzag stitch—curves, corners— also one can see how zigzag and straight stitches have the top thread pulled through to the back, knotted to the back thread and cut, to hold the stitching securely

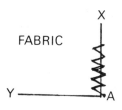

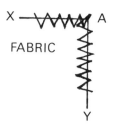

These diagrams show the needle position necessary to make a tidy corner

51 *right* Different appliqué fabrics have been used; hessian background and applied cotton, felt, organdie, etc. Both applied and cut work have been used. Zigzag and straight stitches Amanda Rudolph

52 *below* Appliqué letters with straight stitch Beverly Whitehead

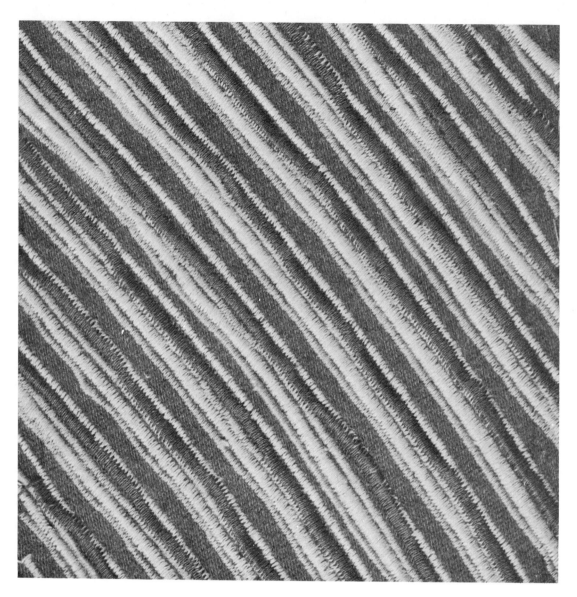

53 *above* and 54 *opposite*
Zigzag and straight stitches
used to makes lines
Audrey Wynne

UNUSUAL FABRICS AND THREADS

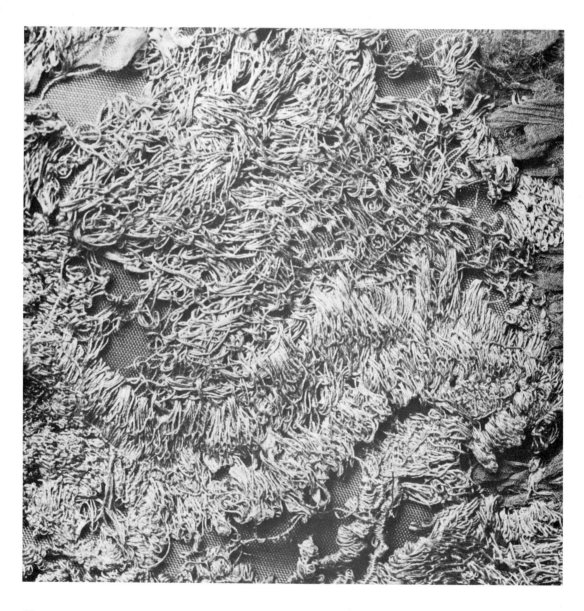

55 *opposite page* Free machining in a frame on an acetate fabric. The work has then been put into acetone and the fabric dissolved leaving this open work effect with the remaining embroidery   Beryl Casey

56 *right* and 57 *below* Thick yarn has been trapped in tubes of polythene. Straight stitch machining on either side make the tubes   Margaret Murray

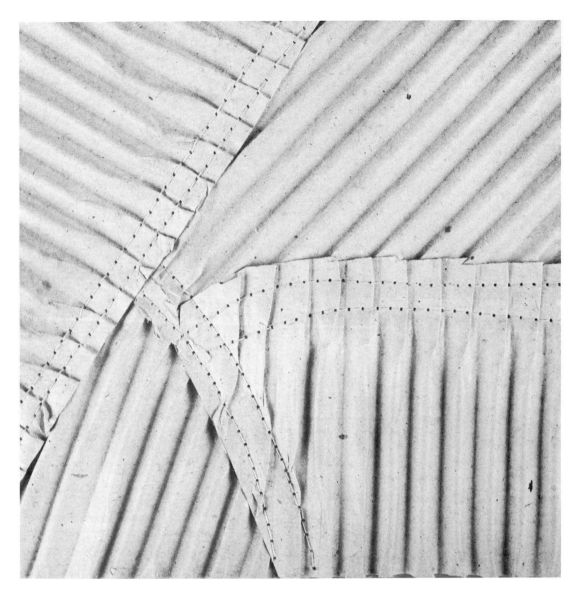

58 *left* and 59 *above*
Straight stitch on a collage
of corrugated paper (note
the machine work flattens
the ridges)
Beverly Whitehead

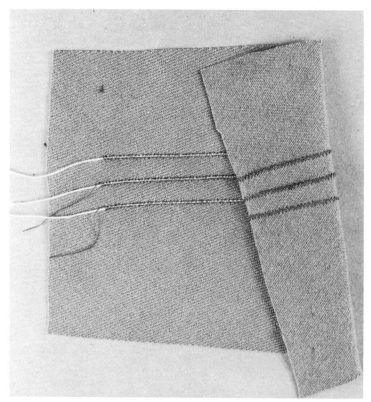

60 and 61 Machine elastic thread. 60 Elastic thread has been put onto the bottom spool by hand. Zigzag stitch. 61 The elastic is drawn up (be careful not to draw it out) to achieve a a sheered effect. 60 back, 61 front

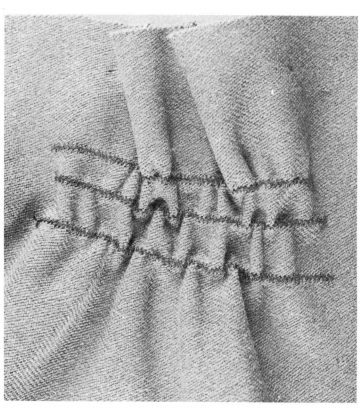

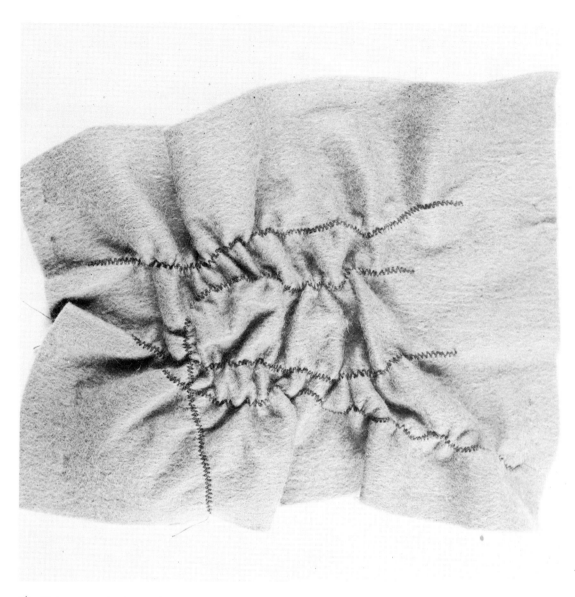

62 This example is made
guiding the elastic on the
top, here the zigzag stitch
is couching the elastic
thread on the right side of
the fabric, the elastic can be
drawn up as the machining
is being done and
afterwards

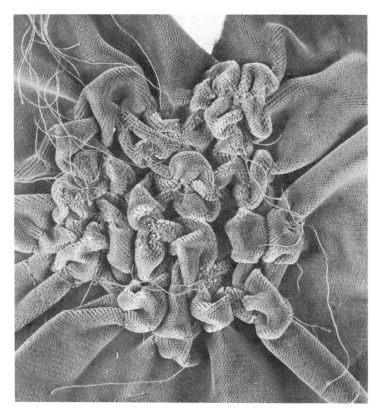

63 The elastic in this example is on the bottom spool and the velvet fabric placed in a frame. A straight stitch has been used, free machining, circular movements made while machining   Beverly Whitehead

64 Again elastic is on the bottom spool but used here on a nylon fabric. The work was not in a frame, zigzag stitch used, free machining

65 A multi-coloured cotton, here red, pale blue, gold, red . . . has been used with a close zigzag stitch in straight rows   Irene Hobson

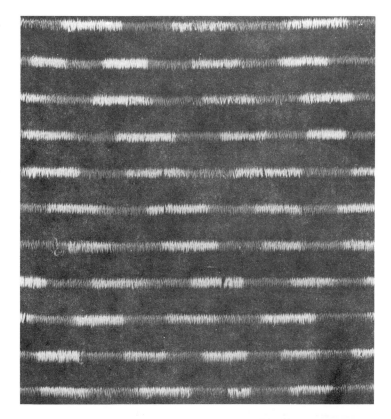

66 A shaded cotton has been used here with a straight stitch, free machining, in a frame Maria Theresa Fernandes

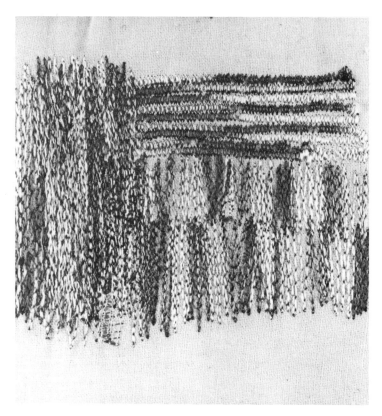

67 A multi-coloured cotton, white, yellow, blue, red. Both straight stitch and zigzag have been used; the straight stitch effect has been made using the reverse and forward lever

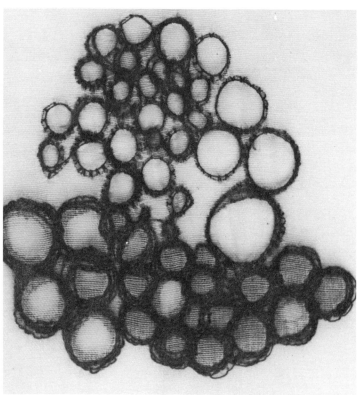

68 Free machining in a frame, using an organdie fabric. The resulting effect is called shadow work. Here the threads at the back of the work can be seen through the organdie (tight lower tension, loose upper tension)

69 A satin fabric has been dyed and quilted (English quilting 86) with rows of straight stitch   Cherilyn Martin

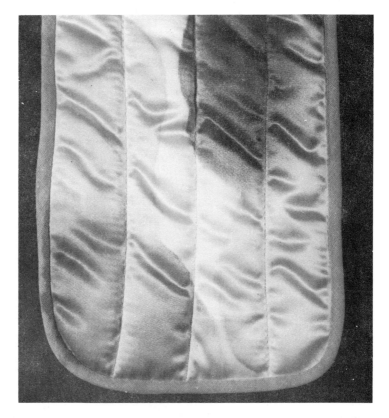

70 A satin fabric has been coloured with fabric crayon, and machined with a straight stitch. The work has been quilted from behind (Trapunto quilting 90)   Geraldine Keating

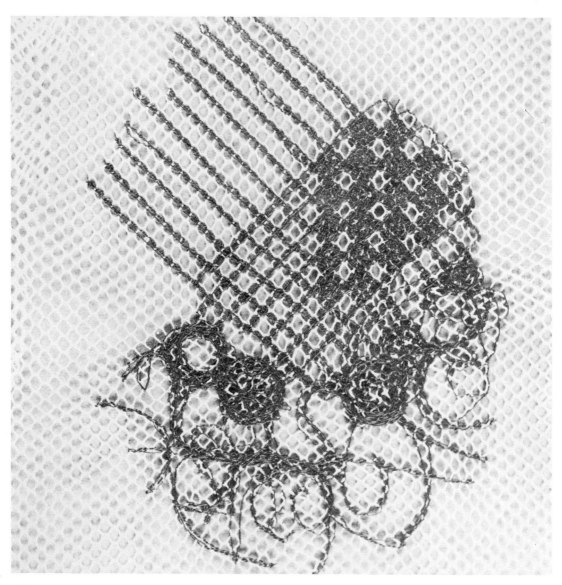

71 *above* Free machining
in a frame on a net fabric.
The tension can obviously
affect the type of line
achieved so it can be
altered to change the
quality of the lines. On the
whole the top tension
should be tightened or
edges usually pull together

72 *opposite* Free machining
in a frame on two layers of
net   Maria Theresa
Fernandes

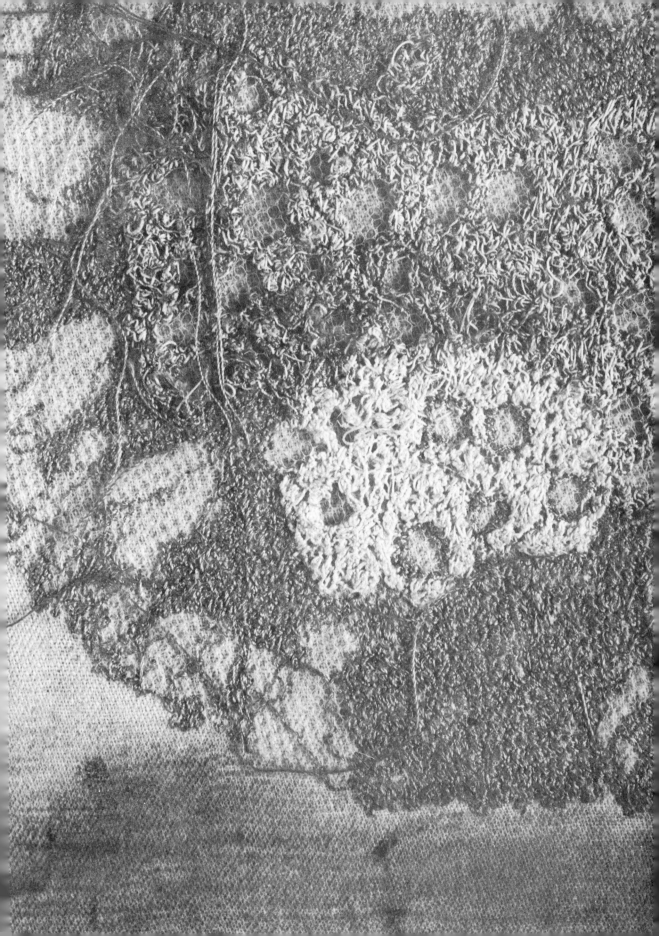

ATTACHMENTS

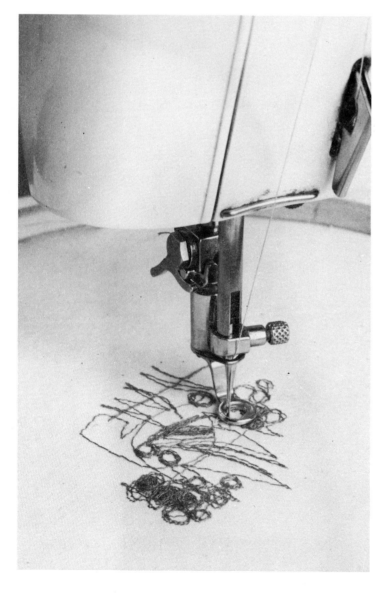

73 Darning foot. Teeth lowered. This foot allows the fabric to be moved freely as the fabric is not held down close by the foot—easy movement, yet it is controlled

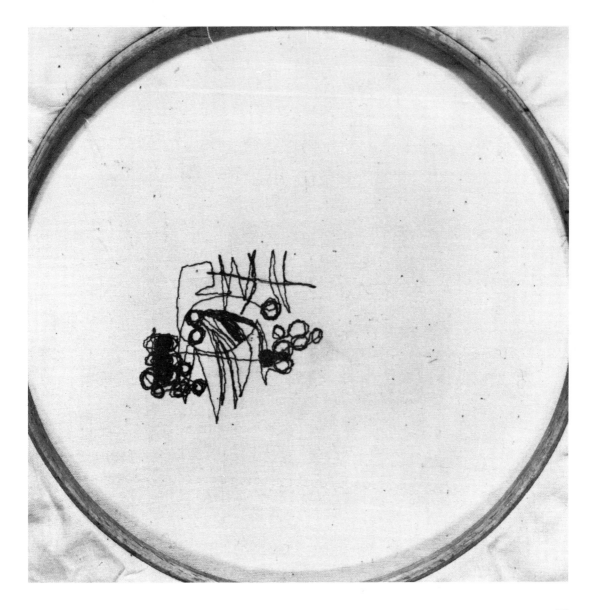

75 *left* and 76 *bottom left* English hole embroidery set (Broderie Anglaise). Lines, curves and holes can be produced

77 *opposite* Stocking Darner attachment. No foot, teeth dropped, straight stitch. A hole has been cut in the fabric, horizontal and vertical lines made and then areas worked to make a pattern.

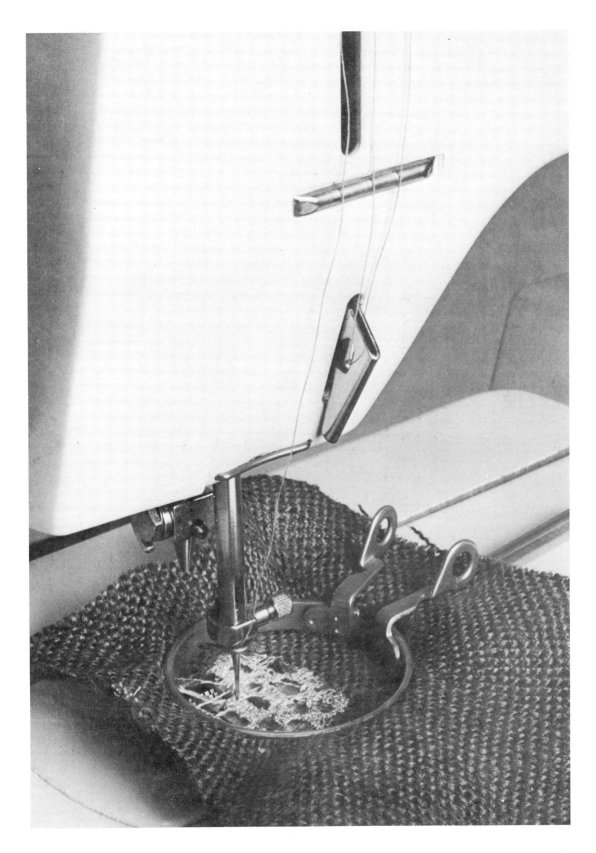

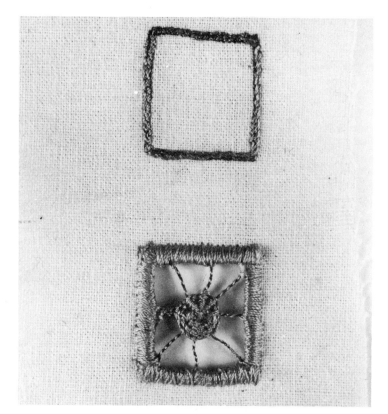

78 *left* and **79** *bottom left*
Cut work, free machining in
a frame or using stocking
darner attachment. 78
shows stages 1 and 7. 79
shows stages 1 to 7. Stage
1—the square is made with
2/3 rows of straight stitch.
Stage 7—a zigzag stitch has
been worked around the
edge

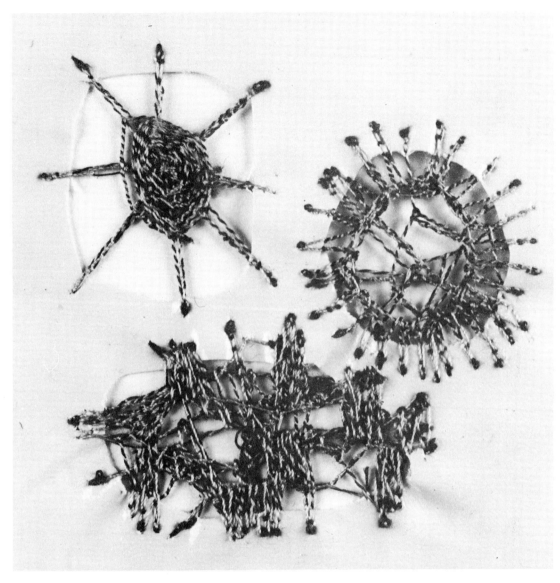

80 A free use of cut work
on a PVC background.

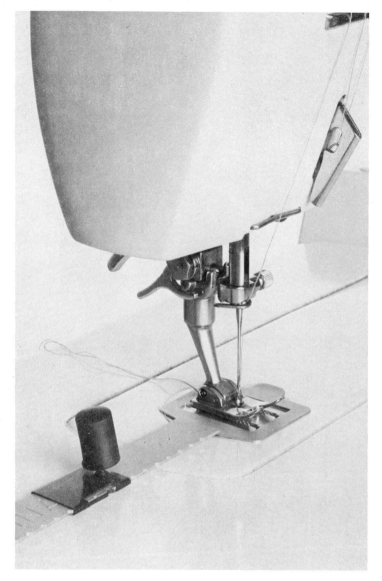

81 *left* Circular embroidery attachment with an ordinary foot. Straight stitch or zigzag can be used. The fabric is moved around in a circular movement by the teeth

82 *opposite* Circular embroidery attachment. Three layers of fabric, from the top, calico, wadding, calico. The firmer the fabric the easier the fabric moved around. NB the rubber cap seen in 81 would normally be placed on the point seen in the centre of 82 above. It has not been put on so the whole process could be seen

83 The machine is set as for example in 82, except the circles are not always completed and the centre point has been changed several times so that the curves cross each other

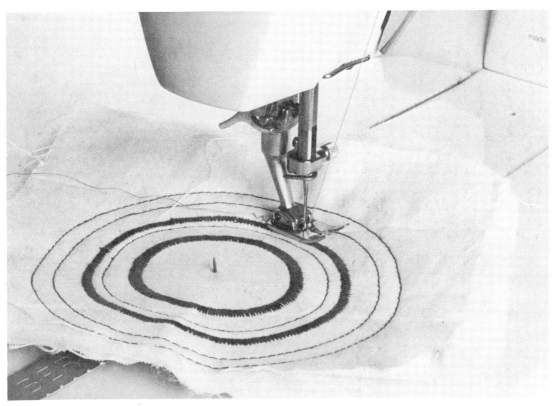

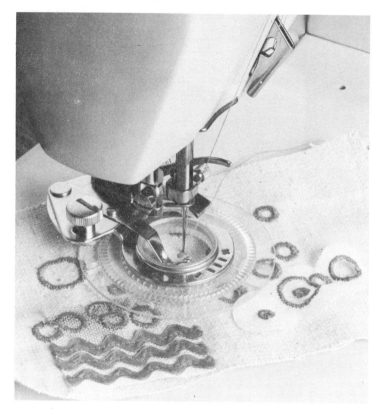

84 *left* Japanese circular sewing attachment: there are two, one with a high lift and another with a low lift, so it can fit any machine. Some machines also need an adaptor as used in this example. Different sizes of circle can be made by adjusting the attachment

85 *below* These are the effects which can be made using Japanese Circular sewing attachment. Threads have been threaded through the holes and fabric pushed through them. On the far right, shisha glass has been placed. These could be put behind the holes

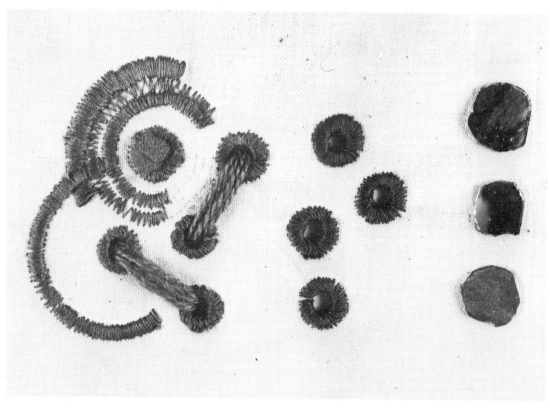

86 *right* Button hole.
Instructions are usually given
with each machine as to the
best way to make them on
that machine

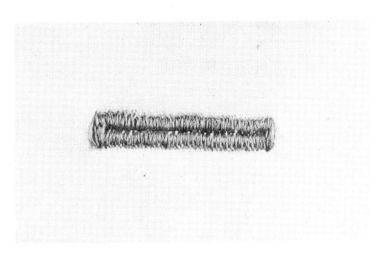

87 *below* Button holes
used to thread ribbon
through; of course smaller
ones could be made, other
materials and threads
threaded through, complex
patterns made with them

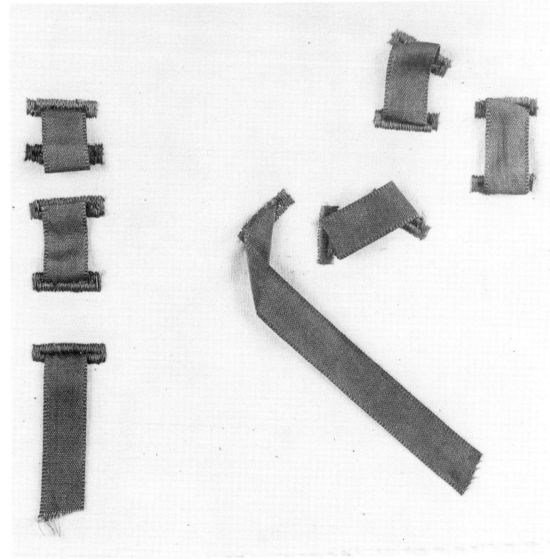

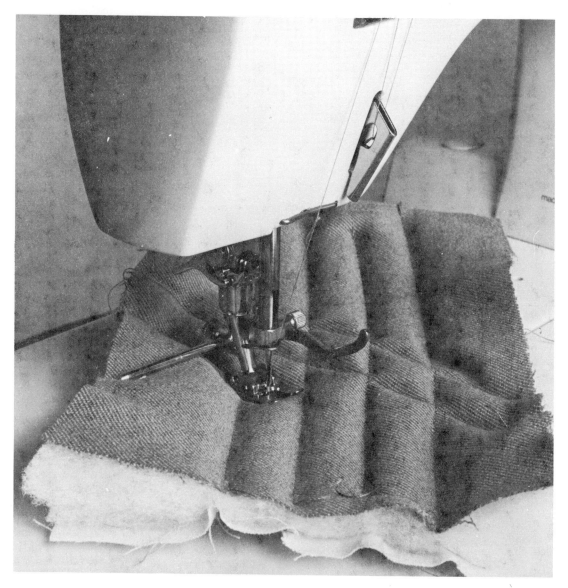

88 Embroidery foot with
guide. The guide is used to
get the distance between
the lines correct. Use with
simple designs. Three layers
of fabric, from the top,
cotton, wadding, calico
fabrics

89 *right* front, 90 *bottom right* back. English quilting using an embroidery foot with guide. Three layers of fabric are required—fabric, wadding and backing fabrics. The fabrics are tacked together so they will not slip. Straight stitch machining, produces a very depressed quilt   Amanda Rudolph

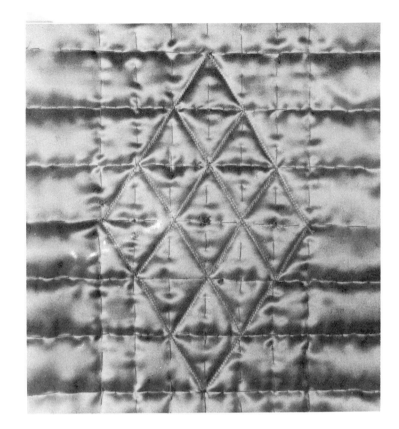

91 *left* front, 92 *bottom left* back. Italian quilting. Two layers of fabric, the top fabric and a backing. A twin needle and a straight stitch. The lines are raised by the double stitching lines being filled with Italian quilting thread   Amanda Rudolph

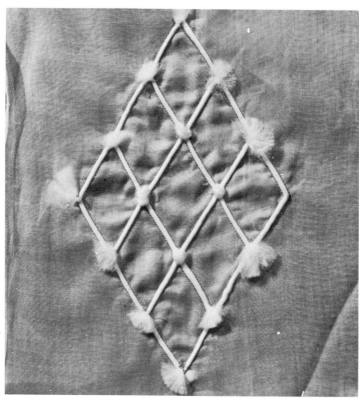

93 *right* front, 94 *bottom right* back. Trapunto quilting. Two layers of fabric, top fabric and backing. The backing fabric has been slit behind each diamond and filled with wadding and over sewn. Each area filled then becomes raised   Amanda Rudolph

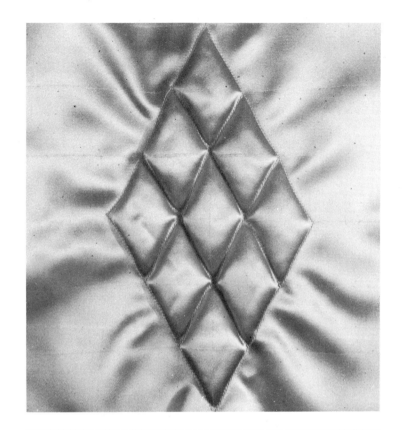

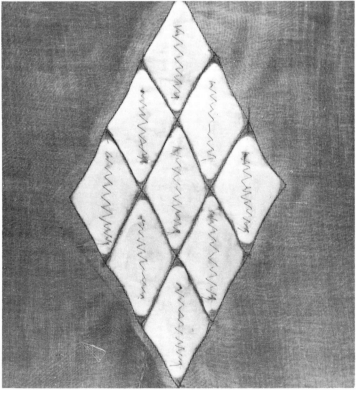

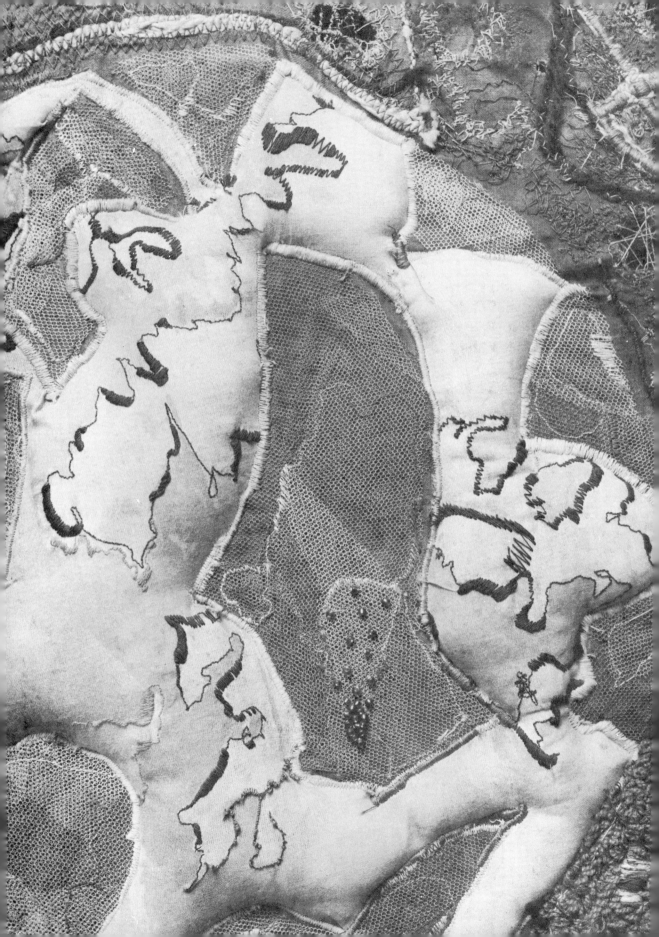

96 *above* Button sewing foot. Zigzag stitch, teeth lowered, needle position left, stitch width can be tested by turning the handle by hand first and adjusted to fit the button

95 *left* Trapunto quilting used in the detail of a panel
Petra Seed

97 *above* Piping foot. Bias
strips of fabric have been cut
for piping, the strip placed
around the cord, tacked, and
tacked into place ready for
machining. There are two
sizes of piping foot. Be sure
to use the correct size of
cord with the foot being
used

98 *opposite* Here the
example being machined in
97 is opened out. An
ordinary seam and piping in
a seam can be seen
together

99 Here is shown two
lengths of fabric out on the
bias, ready to be joined and
used for piping. The piping
is shown clearly. It fits into
a seam and can also be an
edging

100 *above* Embroidery
foot. Zigzag machining on a
canvas. Cotton and silver
thread have been used here

101 *opposite top* and 102
opposite right Machine
embroidery zigzag stitch on
a dyed canvas

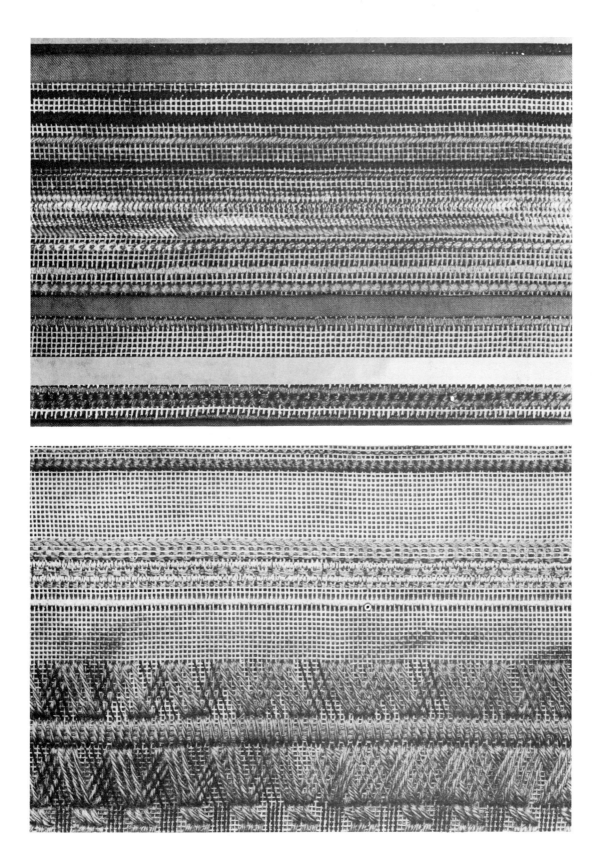

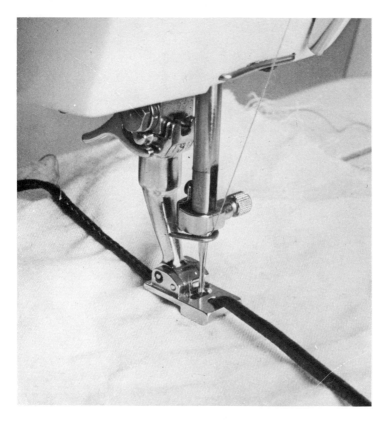

103 *left* Braiding foot. This is used for putting small braids down, like Russia braid, with a straight stitch. The braid is put through the hole in the foot first and then machined down

104 *below* Using a braiding foot, strips of fabric and rug wools held down with a straight stitch

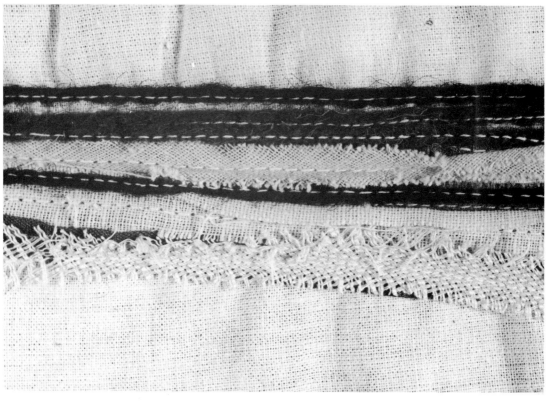

105 Double sided zipper
foot. The needle is set here
to the left treating the pins
like the metal in a zip.
Straight stitch or zigzag can
be used

106 Patterns can be
produced or an irregular pile
with fabric and/or thread.
A A row of threads zigzagged
down as in 105. B Effect
achieved after several rows
of A. C Same method with
strip of fabric

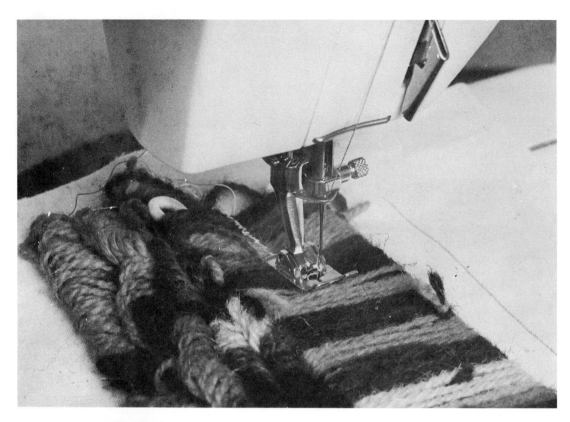

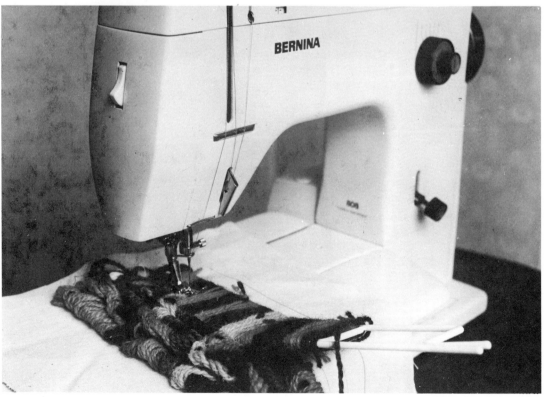

107 *left* and 108 *bottom left* The Elna Rug Fork and zigzag foot. Wind wool or strips of fabric around fork as in 2. Use a close zigzag stitch to hold threads down well. When machining reaches rise in the fork leave the needle in the fabric and ease off about a quarter of the thread on the fork, wind more thread on the fork and slide it down to the flat area, continue—join new colours or threads with a knot in the thread. It can be seen in 107 and 108 how previous rows are flattened to work the next row

109 *above* An area of the pile worked in 107 and 108. Lines are marked out first so the required pile is achieved. Here the pile is cut in parts and left in others

110 *left* Tailor tacking foot. For this foot the top tension must be tightened and zigzag stitch used

111 *below* Tailor tacking foot—change in the stitch length changes the effect of the stitch. (Reverse tends to gather the fabric.) Some of the possibilities can be seen in this example

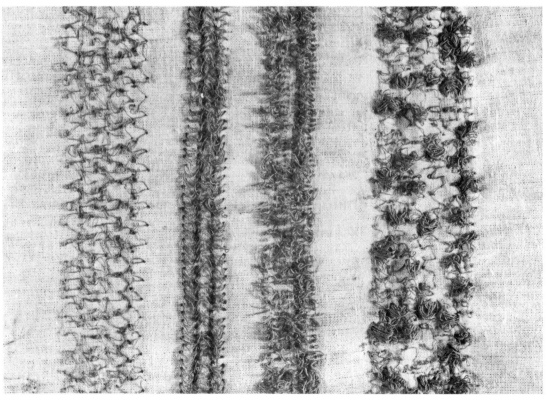

112 *right* Vari-overlock
foot. Here used to oversew
an organdie fabric

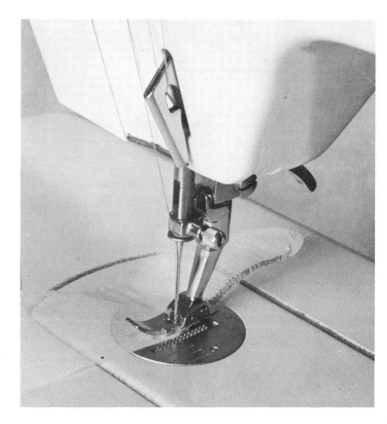

113 *below* Example of
strips of cotton and organdie
overlocked into the fabric,
and off the fabric, and
applied

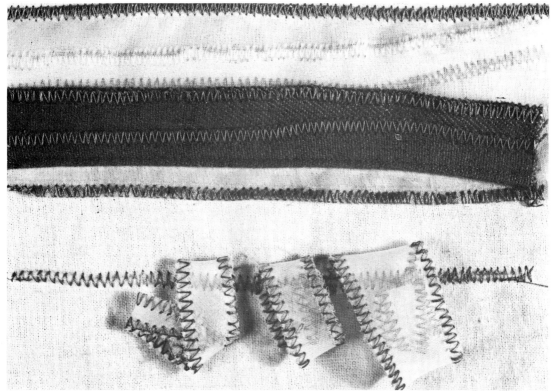

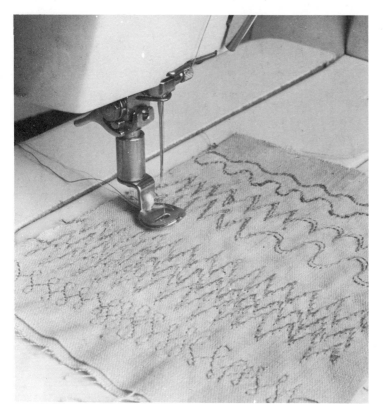

114 Wool darning foot. Teeth lowered. This can be used as seen or used with a frame. It can also be used over a hole in the fabric, for appliqué, and to work over a wool guided automatically when laid into the slot in the foot

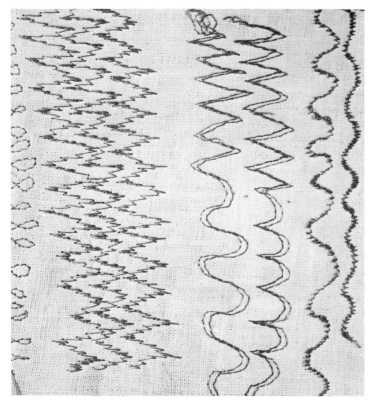

115 Wool darning foot. Left side, zigzag stitch, single needle and the fabric moved from side to side. Right side, the needle has been changed to a double needle and two colours of cotton thread used (a variegated cotton is also very effective)

116 *right* No foot—free
machining with a frame. (A
frame can be used, the
fabric not taut in the frame).
116 and 117 *bottom right*
a loose hessian fabric is
being used so the threads of
the fabric are drawn together
by the machining

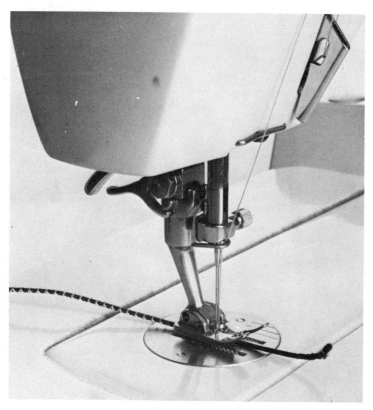

118 *left* Zigzag presser foot. Zigzag stitch over wire, the wire has to be eased through while it is being machined

119 *below* Zigzag presser foot. Zigzag stitch used across the gap of the bent wire to fill the area

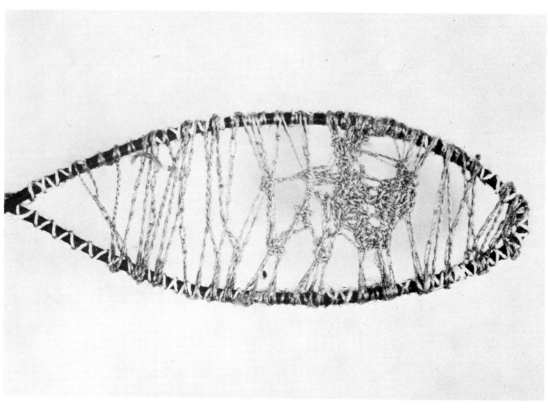

120 Hemmer foot. Straight
stitch. There are various
hemmer feet: for sewing
hems, also a roll and shell
hemmer foot for making a
shell edge or rolled hem.
All can be used to make
effects which can be used
as in example 121

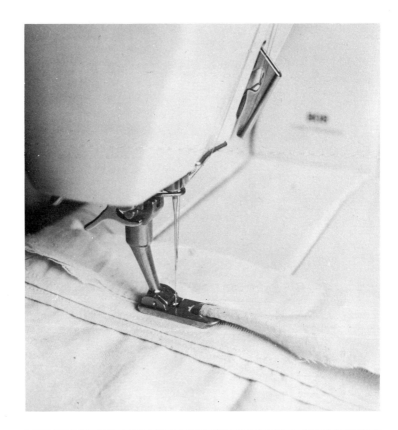

121 The example being
made in 120, cut up and
used with other fabrics

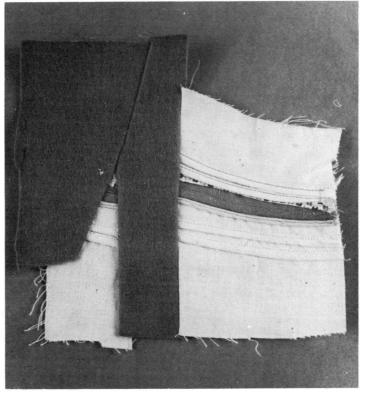

It is important in this section to realize these effects cannot be achieved with just any fabric. Also the grooves in the feet are to keep the work parallel, so the right foot must be used with the right needle. There is a limit to the width of the zigzag before it hits the plate.

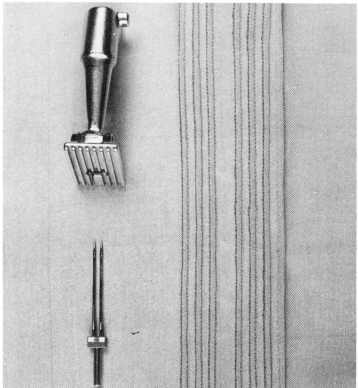

124 *above* Triple needle: an organdie fabric with braid and wool appliqué. Straight stitch and zigzag have been used, and at times three colours

123 *left* Three groove foot and 4 mm Twin needle

124 Seven groove foot and
2 mm Twin needle.
Organdie fabric, straight
stitch and zigzag with two
colours of different thread

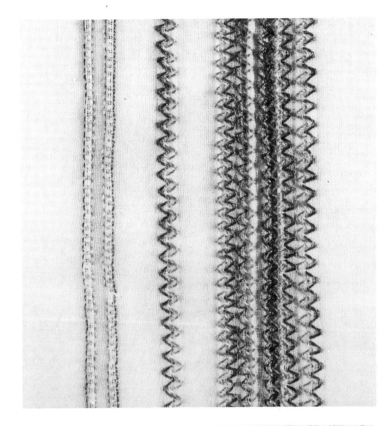

125 Three groove foot and
4 mm needle. A cotton
fabric background with
straight stitch and zigzag
machine work, two colours
of thread

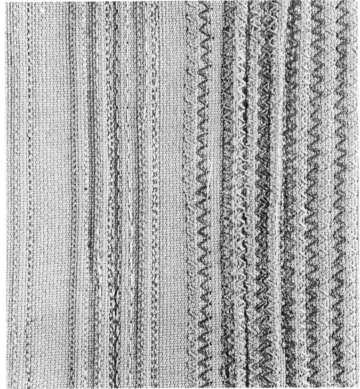

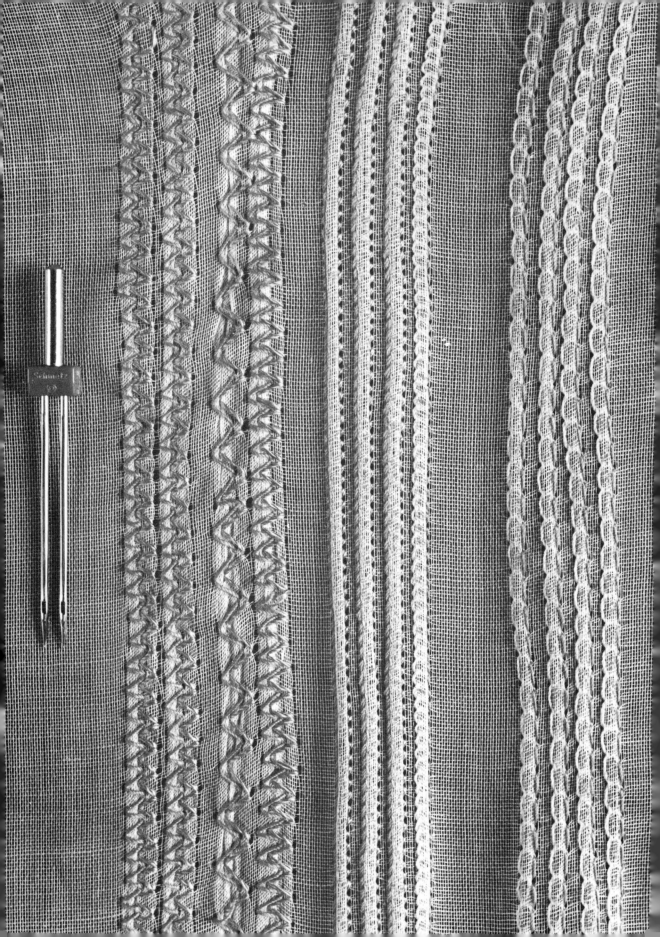

126 Effects have been achieved here varying the tension, straight stitch and zigzag. Twin needles, ordinary foot

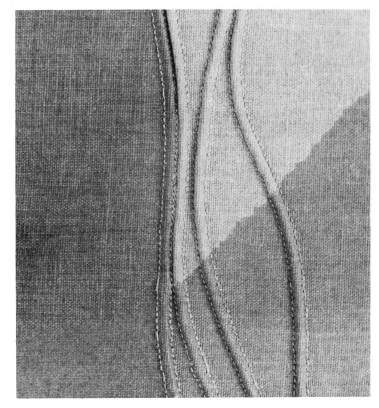

127 *right* Twin needles, ordinary foot, cotton fabric and a straight stitch

128 *right* Twin needles machining, ordinary foot. This has strengthened the fabric so that the detached leaf shapes do not flop Katherine Shaw

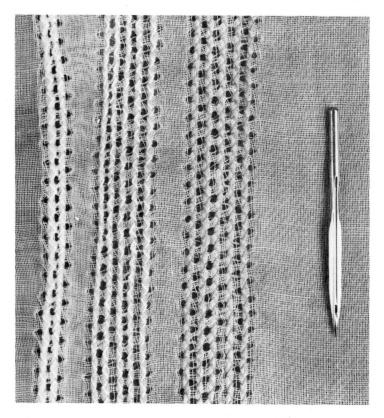

129 Single hemstitch needle, ordinary foot, on an organdie with a zigzag stitch. The effect here is very dependent on the fabric used —and organdie or glazed cotton are easiest to obtain —the closer the weave the better. If a certain fabric must be used it can be sprayed with a starch so that needles in 129 and 130 can be effective

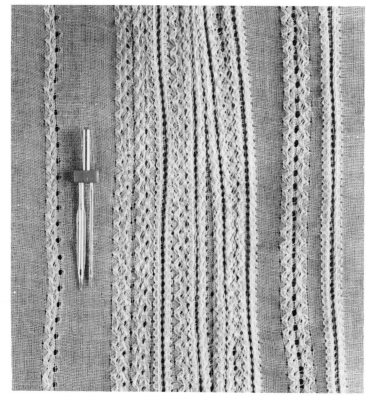

130 Double hemstitch needle, ordinary foot, on an organdie with straight stitch and zigzag machining

SUPPLIERS IN GREAT BRITAIN

For threads and cottons

J & P Coats (UK) Ltd
59 Knowsley Street, Manchester M8 8JX
Atlas machine cotton, thread No 5

C and F Handicraft (Supplies) Ltd
346 Stag Lane, Kingsbury, London NW9 9AG
DMC gold and silver thread for the bobbin, and machine embroidery cotton. Supplied through stockists; the firm will put you in touch with the nearest stockist

MacCulloch & Wallis Ltd
25/26 Dering Street, London W1R 0BH
Various types of machine embroidery cottons

Silken Strands
31 Park Crescent, Furness Vale, Stockport SK12 7PU
Capstan machine embroidery thread

Stephen Simpson Ltd
Avenham Works, Preston PR1 3UR
Fine Lurex silver and gold as a top thread. Will supply direct to the public

J Henry Smith Ltd
Park Road, Calverton, Nottingham NG14 6LL
Machine embroidery thread No. 30, and gold and silver machine thread. Will supply direct to the public

For most of the other equipment—frames, special fabrics, etc

Fred Aldous Handicrafts
37 Lever Street, Manchester M60 1UX

MacCulloch & Wallis Ltd
25/26 Dering Street, London W1R 0BH

The Needlewoman Shop
146–148 Regent Street, London W1

Elizabeth Tracy
Pathfields House, 45 High Street, Haslemere, Surrey

The machine used for this book is a Bernina.
Central office
Bernina Domestic and Industrial Sewing Machines
(Bogod Machine Co Ltd), 50–52 Great Sutton Street
London EC1.

SUPPLIERS IN THE USA
Threads and embroidery accessories

American Thread Corporation
90 Park Avenue, New York

Bucky King Embroideries Unlimited
121 South Drive, Pittsburgh Pennsylvania 15238

The Needle's Point Studio
7013 Duncraig Court, McLean, Virginia 22101

The Rusty Needle
1479 Glenneyre, Laguna Beach, California 92651

Joan Toggitt
1170 Broadway, New York, NY 10001

Yarn Depot
545 Sutter Street, San Francisco 95102

BOOK LIST

Gray, Jennifer MACHINE EMBROIDERY TECHNIQUE
AND DESIGN, Batsford London 1973; Branford Massachusetts
Risley, Christine MACHINE EMBROIDERY, Studio
Vista London 1969
Risley, Christine CREATIVE EMBROIDERY, Studio
Vista London 1973
Dillemont, Thérese de ENCYCLOPEDIA OF NEEDLE-
WORK Mulhouse France DMC. Short section on
machine embroidery.

INDEX